SUPER CUTE CIRCUS ACTIVITY BOOK

Krystin Railing
Big Top Inc.

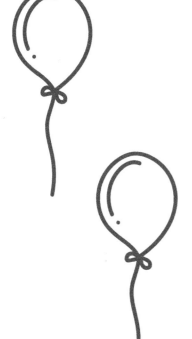

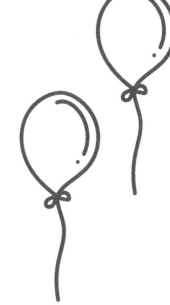

Super Cute Circus Activity Book
Big Top Inc.

Krystin Railing
Lead Designer and Illustrator

Joey Dorsett
Editing and Formatting

With over 10 years of experience in the circus arts and a passion for whimsical designs, Krystin Railing has brought countless characters to life. Her unique style blends vibrant colors with intricate details, captivating young readers and sparking their imagination.

About the Super Cute Circus Activity Book

The Super Cute Circus Activity Book is a delightful journey into the magical world of the circus. Designed for children aged 4-8, this activity book is packed with fun puzzles, coloring pages, and interactive games that encourage creativity and learning.

Inspiration Behind the Book:

The idea for the Super Cute Circus Activity Book came from a childhood love for circuses and a desire to create something that would entertain and educate. The circus is a place of wonder and excitement, and this book aims to capture that feeling with every page.

Design Process:

Creating the Super Cute Circus Activity Book was a labor of love. From brainstorming ideas to creating unique characters and designing each activity, every step was focused on making the book as engaging and enjoyable as possible. The goal was to create a product that both parents and children would love to explore together.

Contact and Follow:

Website: http://www.bigtopinc.com
Instagram: @bigtopinc https://www.instagram.com/bigtopinc
Email: bigtopinc@gmail.com

Thank you for joining us on this whimsical adventure! We hope the Super Cute Circus Activity Book brings as much joy to your family as it did to create it.

WELCOME

TO THE CIRCUS

All About Me

MY NAME IS...

MY AGE

MY BIRTHDAY

MY PET

MY FAVORITE COLOR

MY FAVORITE FOOD

I REALLY LIKE...

Draw a Circus Tent

YOUR CIRCUS STORY

You can write or draw a story!

In the boxes below, share your story! What important events have happened in your life? What are your strongest memories? What hobbies or passions are important to you?

- Where were you born?
- I find it hard to....
- When I was little....
- My favourite thing to do is...
- My biggest struggle has been....
- My biggest success has been....
- I hope that....

MAZE

Can you help the clown get to the circus?

Circus Word Search

Can you find the words hidden in the puzzle?

```
T K C N R H J U G G L E
R H A W R O A H P T U F
A M F O D A N C E R S R
P T U L C K P N C Y I D
E E N C H U L A H O O P
Z R I N G L E A D E R E
E M C O X O R C A F E C
G H Y G M F U N N Y I I
G A C L A T A D D R L J
Y P L B G M Y D C G I U
K P E N I P A U N D S Q
P Y L B C J S A M I M E
```

CLOWN	**MIME**	**UNICYCLE**	**DANCE**
HULA HOOP	**HAPPY**	**CIRCUS**	**TRAPEZE**
FUNNY	**JUGGLE**	**MAGIC**	**RINGLEADER**

CIRCUS
Maze Challenge

Can you help the clown get to the circus?

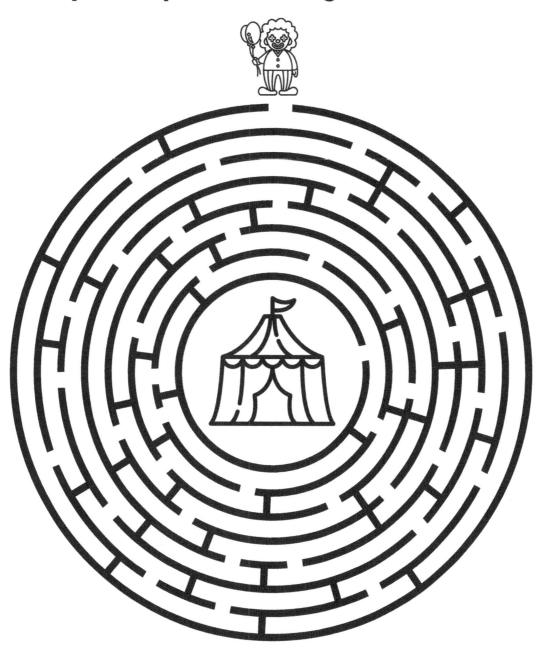

IMAGINATION WORKOUT

Draw each circus character in the corresponding box below.

TIC - TAC - TOE

Be the first player to get three of your marks in a row (horizontally, vertically, or diagonally). One player uses "X" and the other uses "O" Players take turns placing their mark (either "X" or "O") in an empty square. The first player to get three of their marks in a row (horizontally, vertically, or diagonally) wins the game.

TIC - TAC - TOE

Be the first player to get three of your marks in a row (horizontally, vertically, or diagonally). One player uses "X" and the other uses "O". Players take turns placing their mark (either "X" or "O") in an empty square. The first player to get three of their marks in a row (horizontally, vertically, or diagonally) wins the game.

Circus Characters

Look at the pictures and circle the correct words that match the image

Draw a Clown

Circle the Circus Characters

WRITE A CIRCUS STORY

Dots

Dots is a fun game where each player takes a turn connecting one dot to another adjacent dot either horizontally or vertically. Each player takes one move at a time drawing a line. Eventually the board starts to fill with lines. Some will be connected and some not. When you can add a final line to forms a square, fill in the box with your initial and take another turn. The objective is to have the most boxes with your initials.

Dots

Dots is a fun game where each player takes a turn connecting one dot to another adjacent dot either horizontally or vertically. Each player takes one move at a time during a line. Eventually the board starts out with lines. Some will be connected and some not. When you can add a final line to form a square (☐) to the box, you win. Initial and take another turn. The objective is to have the most boxes with your initials.

UNSCRAMBLE

UNSCRAMBLE ALL THE WORDS. GIVE YOURSELF 1 POINT FOR EACH WORD UNSCREMBLED.

POINTS

1. CSIURC TTNE _____ _____

2. LCWON _____ _____

3. UJGLRGE _____ _____

4. HEALENTP _____ _____

5. IGRN AELERD _____ _____

6. RIGET _____ _____

7. NOORTCIONT _____ _____

8. ZTRPEEA _____ _____

9. ENICCLUY _____ _____

10. TILST LWARKE _____ _____

11. RAOLUSEC _____ _____

12. ERIFSR EWHLE _____ _____

13. OTCONT NACYD _____ _____

14. UFNYN _____ _____

15. AAGINCIM _____ _____

TOTAL _____

CIRCUS QUIZ

How much do you know about the circus?
Read and choose the correct options and find out!

1 A circus is performed under a ___
 a) Bed
 b) Tent
 c) Car

2 Who is in charge of running the show at the circus?
 a) Clown
 b) Tiger
 c) Ring Leader

3 What is a common prop used by clowns to entertain the audience?
 a) Balloons
 b) Swords
 c) Books

4 Which performer is known for throwing multiple objects at once?
 a) Acrobat
 b) Juggler
 c) Dancer

5 Who bends and flexes their body into unusual and extreme positions?
 a) Aerialist
 b) Contortionist
 c) Clowns

6 What act performs high above the ground?
 a) Hula Hooper
 b) Trapeze
 c) Contortionist

7 Which animal is associated with circus performances?
 a) Dog
 b) Cat
 c) Elephant

8 Which performer is known for comedy and exaggerated makeup?
 a) Ring Leader
 b) Juggler
 c) Clown

9 Which performers create human pyramids and balance on each other?
 a) Jugglers
 b) Acrobats
 c) Aerialists

10 What is small vehicle used by clowns to perform humorous acts?
 a) Skate Board
 b) Unicycle
 c) Roller Skates

Made in the USA
Middletown, DE
13 January 2025